‖‖‖‖‖‖‖‖‖‖‖
I0142255

A Psychic Life

Living with Extraordinary Perception

Terri Branson

Non-Fiction from
Dragonfly Publishing, Inc.

* * * * *

CHAPTER 1

Defining Psychic

WHAT is a psychic?

In the simplest terms, a psychic is considered someone with abilities beyond the normal five senses of *sight, hearing, taste, touch,* and *smell.* That includes perceiving and dealing with spiritual realms, seeing past and future, and even affecting the natural world through subtle energies.

By that definition, am I psychic? Yes.

Does being psychic affect my life? Yes.

Being different from the average person is challenging for anyone. Being psychic in a world where a vast majority of people are not presents a unique set of challenges.

Imagine walking down the electronics aisle of a retail department store where someone has turned on every radio on display and set each one to a different channel. The result is a cacophony, where picking one stream out of many is difficult to impossible.

That is how someone with psychic ability feels walking into a crowded room. Thoughts, emotions, memories, feelings, mental images, and more pelt like a hail storm of information.

Often the temptation to run screaming is too strong to ignore, and sometimes a judicious exit is the wisest course of action.

A life filled with psychic phenomena can be challenging, but also very interesting.

The trick is to understand how to deal with all of that additional information, while creating a workable niche.

* * * * *

Chakra Chart

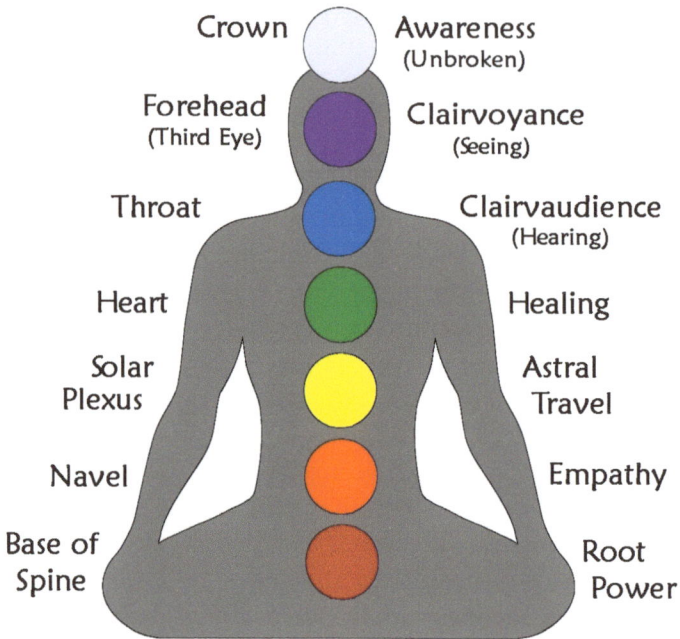

ABILITY	ZONE	COLOR	NOTE
Root Power	Spinal Base	Red	C (Do)
Empathy	Navel	Orange	D (Re)
Astral Travel	Solar Plexus	Yellow	E (Mi)
Healing	Heart	Green	F (Fa)
Hearing	Throat	Blue	G (Sol)
Seeing	Forehead	Indigo	A (La)
Awareness	Top of Head	Lavender	B (Ti)

CHAPTER 2

Chakras by Function

THE term chakra is the most accurate and functional way I know to explain the basic psychic zones.

There are seven chakras. Each is associated with a color, a note on the musical scale, and an ability.

The chakras correspond in order with both color and sound as: root power (drawing ambient energy into the body), empathy (sensing emotions), astral travel (walking in the spirit realm), healing (sharing energy), hearing (clairaudience or telepathy), seeing (clairvoyance), and awareness (unbroken consciousness).

There are seven primary notes on a musical scale that correspond with the seven primary colors in a rainbow. Each color has a matching sound frequency that corresponds with abilities beyond the five senses. Red corresponds with middle-C (Do), and so on up the C-scale, like this: Do (Red), Re (Orange), Mi (Yellow), Fa (Green), Sol (Blue), La (Indigo), Ti (Lavender).

Most people learn psychic abilities in rainbow order from red to lavender. Psychic ability is about knowledge that resides within the soul (or spirit), not in the genetics of a body. The body into which one incarnates has nothing to do with extrasensory abilities.

Psychic abilities are spiritual tools learned over many lifetimes through much trial and error. For example, a person might be empathic with the ability to draw root power energy, but cannot yet manage astral travel nor have any ability up the chakra color chart.

There are exceptions, however, where someone has a strong ability up the chart but no mastery of abilities lower on the chart. People with abilities skipped across chakra zones tend to live very difficult lives.

The ideal is to master each chakra zone in order from root power up to unbroken awareness.

* * * * *

First Chakra

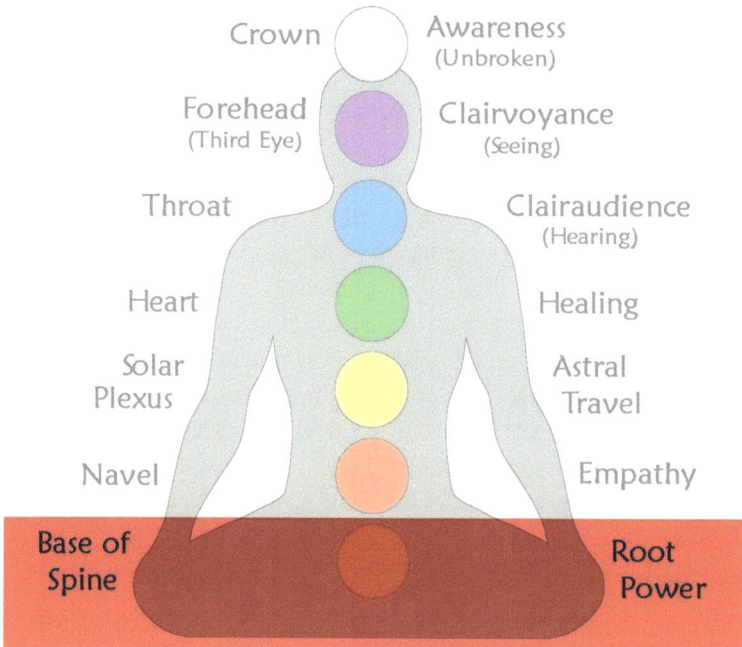

Root Power
Location: Base of Spine
Associated Color: Red
Musical Note: C (Do)

CHAPTER 3

Tapping into Power

THE first chakra is the root, the base. It is associated with the color red and the musical note C (Do).

The base chakra is used for tapping into ambient energy in the world around you.

Never steal energy from other living things, not even plants. That is wrong and karma will catch up with you for such acts. No matter how much you tell yourself that your immediate need outweighs any violation against another living entity, it is still a violation.

All around you there is an endless ebb and flow of subtle energy fields. Psychic-101 meets Physics-101 in the world of quantum space. They deal with the same energies, only under different terminology.

Energy is energy, whether you tap into it with your mind or funnel it into a battery to run a mechanical device.

In fact, people are complex organic machines, which operate on energy fields like everything else in the universe.

The discipline of meditation helps put you in touch with those subtle energy fields, so you can be in tune with your surroundings and at the same time replenish your energy reserves.

Tapping into base root energy should be a natural and simple process. It should not hurt, such as giving you a headache. Neither should it give you a buzz or rush of any kind. It should flow through you in an easy stream.

* * * * *

Second Chakra

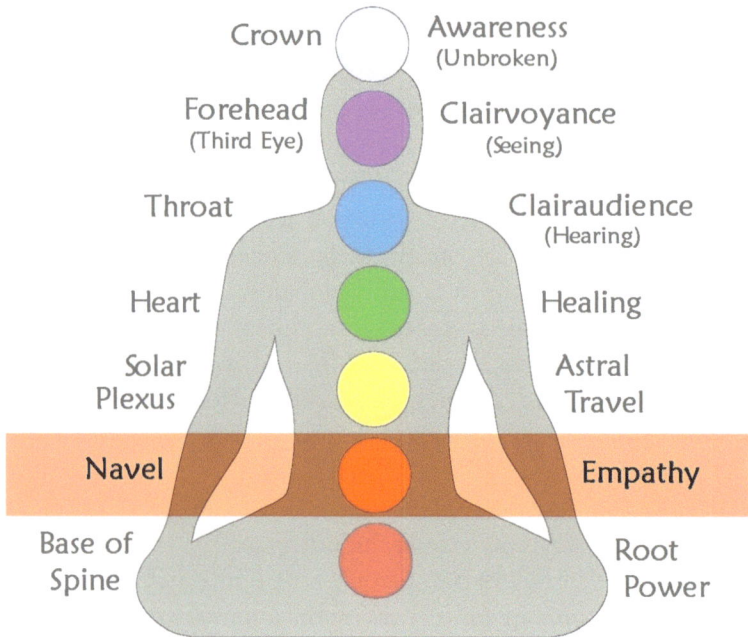

Empathy
Location: Navel Region
Associated Color: Orange
Musical Note: D (Re)

CHAPTER 4

Sifting Emotions

THE second chakra is empathy. It is associated with the color orange and the musical note D (Re).

Empathy is the ability to sense the emotions of other people, animals, and even plants. From joy to sadness, safety to fear, emotional streams waft through the atmosphere like sound waves. The soul functions as a radio tuner, surfing along wavelengths to find songs of interest.

Learn to tune out the feelings of those around you, even shut them off completely when necessary. Living without any emotion is a lonely existence, but being able to control the inflow of empathic data as needed is a necessary skill to master.

You don't experience someone else's feelings in the same way they do. Rather, you pick up information as a kind of mental *weather report*. An empathic wave can hit like a strong gust of wind, prickling dry or wet, hot or cold, soothing or grating, welcoming or repelling. You taste emotions in your mind, but certain empathic waves can also produce a physical affect on the body.

Have you ever walked into a room and felt nobody wanted you in there? Somehow you just *knew* someone in that room wanted you gone. Most of the time, you are happy to oblige where possible. Choosing to stay and fight can be fraught with complications, because you are opting to acknowledge that you sense the feelings of others around you. Some people do not like that and can panic, if they realize you are tapping into their experiences on the spot.

The old saying "discretion is the better part of valor" is in full force when dealing with the emotions of others. Direct confrontation can be useful and sometimes entertaining from a mischievous point of view, but it also can be dangerous. Sift emotions, like flour through a mesh strainer. Throw out the stuff you don't like. Keep what you do like. Learn to slow down the flow to a manageable rate and to maintain privacy.

* * * * *

Third Chakra

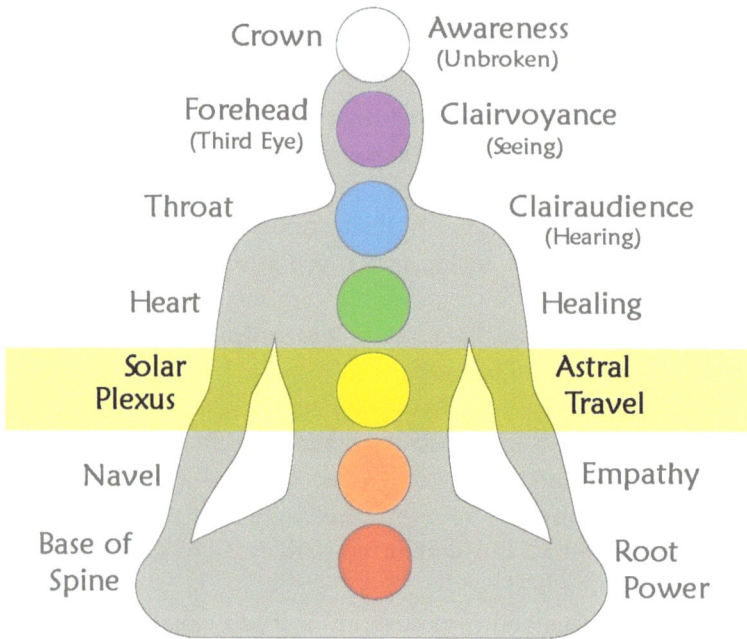

Crown — Awareness (Unbroken)
Forehead (Third Eye) — Clairvoyance (Seeing)
Throat — Clairaudience (Hearing)
Heart — Healing
Solar Plexus — Astral Travel
Navel — Empathy
Base of Spine — Root Power

Astral Travel
Location: Solar Plexus
Associated Color: Yellow
Musical Note: E (Mi)

CHAPTER 5

Spiritual Journeys

THE third chakra is astral travel. It is associated with the color yellow and the musical note E (Mi).

Mastering astral travel requires discipline, calm, and lots of practice. There are no shortcuts or quick routes for learning this useful and powerful skill. There are those who practice astral travel as a separation experience, where the body is left in one place while the spirit travels elsewhere. I do not advocate that method, because there are just too many dangers associated with it.

The safest method of astral projection is a form of bi-location that creates a wormhole through space and time. This is also known as quantum tunneling. Instead of separating spirit from body, bi-location creates a temporary connection to another point in space and time. When dealing with points in space, you are also dealing with time. You can look across space and try to be in time with a current event. You can also look back in time to observe an event of the past.

Looking forward in time is complicated, because you must make sure to get the right dimensional slice, the right timeline. Otherwise, you are peering into the realm of potential outcomes and have no idea which one flows with your timeline. As a general rule, it is wise to remain skeptical of those who claim to be able to predict the future with any degree of accuracy. Looking forward is a difficult task. Those few who can see into the future only rarely snag snippets in the right dimensional time frame.

Peering into the past, on the other hand, is a simpler exercise. You need to know who, where, and when. Get as many details as you can gather. Then try to locate that point in time and allow it to unfold.

Astral travel, whether to the past or present or future, should be approached with caution. Never assume anything seen or experienced on the astral plane is correct, because getting the right dimensional slice is always tricky.

* * * * *

Fourth Chakra

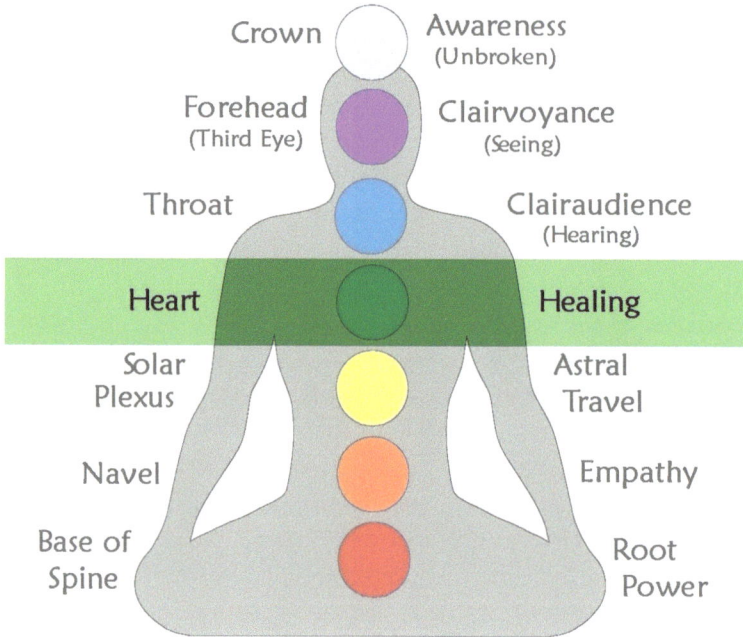

Crown — Awareness (Unbroken)
Forehead (Third Eye) — Clairvoyance (Seeing)
Throat — Clairaudience (Hearing)
Heart — Healing
Solar Plexus — Astral Travel
Navel — Empathy
Base of Spine — Root Power

Healing
Location: Heart
Associated Color: Green
Musical Note: F (Fa)

CHAPTER 6

Healing Energies

THE fourth chakra is the realm of healing. It is associated with the color green and the musical note F (Fa).

The term healing is a bit of a misnomer. The fourth charka is, first and foremost, the zone where energy is transferred from one body to another. In this most basic form, one can help or one can harm.

Doing harm always carries negative consequences. This is why I prefer to think of the fourth chakra as the healing zone, rather than the energy transfer zone.

By the time you reach the fourth chakra, you should be proficient in managing the flow and feel of energy fields. Again, this is about working your way up the energy ladder, learning as you go.

People approach healing in many ways. The most common method is the power of positive thought through prayer and meditation, but there is also the hands-on approach of giving energy through direct physical contact. As a general rule, I advise working from a distance without physical contact. That is the safest method for all concerned, although it is the most difficult.

The best way to offer a positive energy effect is to visualize white or golden light to stimulate at the cellular level. In other words, give a body just enough of an energy boost to heal itself. When you do it that way, healing is more likely to be permanent and not just a temporary patch that could fade with time.

Any transfer of energy from one individual to another can be draining. However, the better you are with managing root energy (first chakra), the easier it is. If done properly, you should not feel drained or distressed.

Always consider the greater good.

Do no harm, and that includes to yourself.

* * * * *

Fifth Chakra

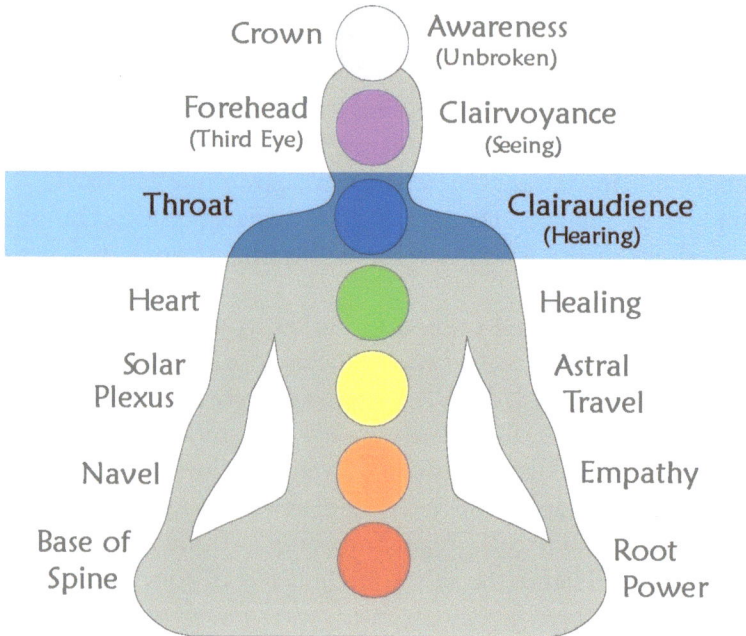

Crown — Awareness (Unbroken)

Forehead (Third Eye) — Clairvoyance (Seeing)

Throat — Clairaudience (Hearing)

Heart — Healing

Solar Plexus — Astral Travel

Navel — Empathy

Base of Spine — Root Power

Hearing (Clairaudience)
Location: Throat
Associated Color: Blue
Musical Note: G (Sol)

CHAPTER 7

Cosmic Radio

THE fifth chakra is the realm of hearing. It is associated with the color blue and the musical note G (Sol).

The chakra of hearing is sometimes referred to as clairaudience. Most people know it by the term telepathy, as in hearing the thoughts of others. That includes people, animals, and anything in the spiritual world with intelligence.

Telepathy occurs quite literally at the speed of light. Once a thought is formed, it can be detected before a person has a chance to speak it. If someone is thinking in rapid fire on complex issues, then what you perceive is an overlapping effect, like one wave intersecting another. You telepathically hear the next thought strand while the person is speaking the previous thought. This can be very confusing.

In a brisk conversation with someone who tends to think very fast, it is often best to concentrate on listening with your ears and tuning out telepathic input. It does not always work and requires a lot of practice. However, if you can master this handy skill, it will make life easier in some situations.

Because telepathy occurs in what some call quantum space, also known more commonly as astral space, communication is not only instantaneous but can occur over vast distances. In fact, once telepathic communication has been established, the distance factor is more or less nullified. It is just as easy to pick up telepathic thoughts across the world as it is across a room. In fact, sometimes it is easier, because there is less local interference. Will telepathy reach out into space? Some say yes, and there is no reason to believe otherwise.

Entering a room that radiates negative thoughts can cause the same type of discomfort as walking into a room ripe with negative feelings. It is always a balancing act of reaction versus inaction. You have the choice to react to something or to ignore it.

Sometimes thoughts are just too hard to ignore and you feel compelled to react to them, to confront the person standing before you.

That can be dangerous, especially if the person is not aware that you can *hear* what they are thinking.

Those who know you well and understand your capabilities should know better than to bait you with their thoughts. I tend to be rather unforgiving of such behavior and usually reward it accordingly.

It is sheer folly for a non-telepathic person to pick a fight of any kind with a telepathic person, be that a mental challenge or a physical fight. Again, telepathy works at the speed of light. In the split second it takes the other person to think something, you can catch that thought and have a counter ready.

One example, be that fair or not, is sports. When I was a kid I played lots of different sports in a tiny rural elementary school. I was not the greatest athlete, but I was a farm girl in good physical condition paired with a nimble mind. One of my favorite tricks to play was to steal the ball from unsuspecting forwards on the basketball court. I simply bent my knees, looked into their eyes, and waited for them to *think* which way they would go. As soon as the basketball rolled off the palm, I stole it before it hit the ground. I either scooped it up to dribble or pass, or took great delight in diverting it forcefully into the stands. Once I got so annoyed with the other basketball team's coach, both with what he was saying and what he was thinking, that I batted a basketball straight into his face. Yep, technical foul. They threw me out of the game for that one. Was it worth it? I hate to admit it, but it was.

More practical applications for telepathy come with the activities of daily life, such as driving a car and being able to anticipate the behavior of nearby drivers. That is a safety factor.

Just about any mundane interaction with other people can yield opportunities to use telepathy to provide deeper understand of your surroundings, resulting in more safety and more information at hand.

* * * * *

Sixth Chakra

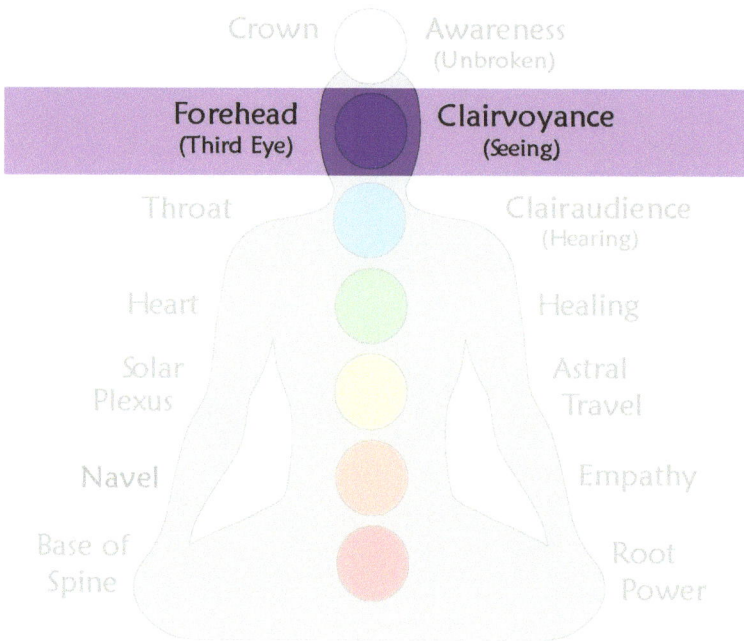

Seeing (Clairvoyance)
Location: Forehead (Third Eye)
Associated Color: Indigo
Musical Note: A (La)

CHAPTER 8

Mental Movies

THE sixth chakra is the realm of seeing with the mind instead of the eyes. It is associated with the color indigo and the musical note A (La).

Clairvoyance is the most common term for this ability, but it is also known third eye sight and remote viewing.

In the simplest terms, you see other places, even other times and realms, with your mind's eye. Such scenes can be a clear as anything observed with physical eyes. Sometimes you can perceive more, because you can adjust to see more angles as needed.

Most of the time all of your senses kick into gear, giving you sight, smells, sounds, feelings, and more. Once you hone in on a scene, you determine how much data you wish to absorb. These are truly mental movies with a kick.

As with telepathy, clairvoyance punches through the restrictions of both time and space, tunneling from one event slice to another.

Distance is not a factor.

Time is not a factor.

However, you must learn how to orient yourself in space and time. Otherwise, you might wind up in the wrong time or the wrong reality. As with any psychic skill, clairvoyance requires practice. You must learn how to queue in on the right place at the right time.

Once you have mastered the skill of clairvoyance, it should be as simple as concentrating on the where and the when. No strange rituals or weird coordinate systems are required. Just point the mind and go.

One aspect of clairvoyance is the ability to skip through time. Going backward in time is not difficult, but it is a skill you must hone. It is just as easy to look back many years, even centuries, as it is to look back a few hours. It takes no more effort, because you are punching through astral space to find a place and a when. You just think it and go there.

Going back in time is easy, but going forward in time presents special difficulties. The main reason is that you must leap forward into the correct reality. Some have claimed to have the ability to predict the future with accuracy. Only a scant few have been documented to have had any real accuracy in looking head in the time. That is because it is very difficult to make sure you stay on your timeline's path.

Going backward in time is easy to trace, because you can sense the path of your own timeline. To look ahead in time, you must know how to stay on the correct dimensional path and not veer into alternate realities.

Glimpses of the future can come unbidden. Usually, predictions come as short dreams, but waking glimpses can occur. Brief forays into the future that occur in a waking state can be confusing and dangerous, because what you experience will eclipse everything going on around you. It is best to train your mind not to take unscheduled trips, while you are awake. Teach yourself to put on those mental brakes.

As a general rule, I discourage attempting to peer into the future. It is safer and better to look into the past, using it to guide you on your journey.

* * * * *

Seventh Chakra

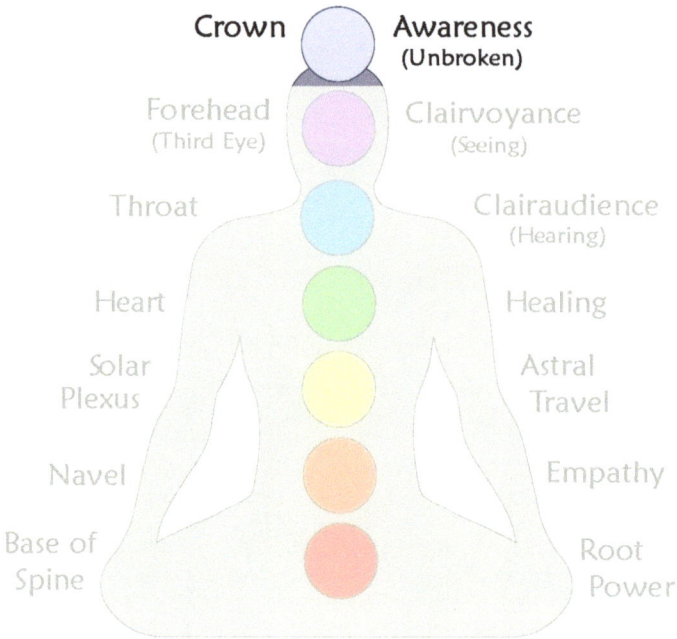

Crown	Awareness (Unbroken)
Forehead (Third Eye)	Clairvoyance (Seeing)
Throat	Clairaudience (Hearing)
Heart	Healing
Solar Plexus	Astral Travel
Navel	Empathy
Base of Spine	Root Power

Unbroken Awareness
Location: Top of Head (Crown)
Associated Color: Lavender
Musical Note: B (Ti)

CHAPTER 9

Unbroken Awareness

THE seventh chakra is the realm of unbroken consciousness. It is associated with the color lavender and the musical note B (Ti).

When someone reaches the level of unbroken consciousness, they in reality are never truly asleep. The body rests in sleep, but the mind keeps working.

This is not a state of half-sleep, where you are resting but not fully asleep. The body is fully asleep, leaving the spirit to work as it will. Sometimes you walk astral realms, while the body sleeps. Other times you work out the issues of life.

A state of unbroken consciousness should only be practiced by those who have mastered all six previous chakras. Without full control over all of the lower chakras, unbroken consciousness can fracture a mind.

It is difficult to explain how unbroken consciousness feels. The best analogy I can give is the difference between doing physical labor and sitting down to read a book. Physical tasks exercise the body and mind in tandem, while mental tasks exercise only the mind.

Those who have reached the level of unbroken consciousness tend to be cranky about their "me time."

Time to rest, both physically and mentally.

Time away from others, away from schedule tasks.

This type of temporary unstructured flow is necessary to give the mind time to rest. It is not a luxury. It is required for good mental and spiritual health.

* * * * *

CHAPTER 10

The Spooky Side

THERE are many kinds of things that go bump in the night.

Things that blur by in the shadows.

Things that walk in the sunlight.

Things that are helpful.

Things that are evil.

How many different kinds of energy things are out there? To be honest, no one knows the totality of the cosmos, but there are some kinds of spirits and energies that can be categorized.

The term "spirits" generally refers to disembodied souls, as in those who have died and presently have no corporeal form. Spirits are not just human. They can be non-human, as well, including animals and other more exotic things. However, as a general rule, most spirits encountered are humans between incarnations.

The term "energies" applies to cohesive energy fields that range from semi-intelligent to non-intelligent. Most semi-intelligent entities are known as elementals, whereas most non-intelligent energies are produced naturally in nature.

An elemental can arise naturally from a geographic location, if enough disparate energies coalesce into a specific spot. Basically, a natural elemental is formed of the residual energies left behind by intelligent creatures and extreme events. Elementals can be created artificially. However, I oppose the purposeful creation of elementals of any kind and believe the energies of such entities should be dispersed without haste.

Elementals of both types, natural and unnatural, can be tricky and dangerous beasts. They rarely have enough intelligence to act beyond their own instincts for survival or whatever directive they have been given. Think of an elemental as a mortally wounded animal in the woods. You don't want to approach it, because it cannot understand that you mean it no harm. Since you cannot help it, as it has no other evolutional state other than to gather more energy and power, the only thing you can do is put it out of its misery. You do that by dispersing its energy. An elemental is nothing more than a cohesive energy field. The safest and kindest way to deal with any elemental you encounter is to interrupt the field bond, thereby releasing its energy harmlessly back into nature.

Earth energies are usually less dangerous than elementals, because they have no inherent intelligence. But they are energy fields and, as such, can present dangers. Consider a spider web. The spider weaves the web for its own purposes, as a home and a trap for food. When the spider is gone, dead or simply moved on elsewhere, the web remains. The web has no inherent intelligence. It just is. And it continues to serve its function as a barrier and a trap. Earth energies tend to be localized energy traps. Any time you encounter one, take the necessary steps to disperse it.

Ghosts are by far the most prevalent entities to encounter. They go by many terms, including souls, spirits, and even shades. The seat of intelligence is the soul. Ghosts are the souls of deceased people. The primary thing to remember is that ghosts can think. Without bodies, thinking is all that is left to them.

Recently deceased spirits can be very confused. Many cannot grasp the fact that they are dead, but they know something is wrong. Reactions vary from denial to horror to anger.

An angry ghost is not a threat, until it learns how to manipulate the energies of the natural world. Once it figures out how to move things in the physical world and how to communicate with people, it can choose to be helpful or dangerous. Ghosts are thinking souls, who make their own decisions on whether to be good or bad.

It takes time and presence of mind for a ghost to learn how to move physical objects and know how to communicate with the living. Usually, ghosts who can move objects and speak with the living are those who have been in spirit form a very long time. There is truth in stories of ancient places with old ghosts that display great power to move physical objects, create audible sounds, and communicate telepathically.

The longer humans inhabit a specific location, the more likely the area is to have old ghosts of great power and even some elementals. You must learn to distinguish between the two in order to manage them.

The primary goal in dealing with any ghost is to figure out why it is lingering and help it move along to the next incarnation. I don't subscribe to the "just learn to live with them" approach. People are not supposed to linger in spirit form. The intention is to move to the next life, go through the tunnel, walk into the light, or whatever metaphor works best for you.

How do you get a ghost to move on to the next life? Sometimes the first thing you have to do is convince them that they have died. Even ones who admit to being dead often can be stubborn or just plain frightened to move to the next phase.

Every person is an individual, including ghosts. That means you must speak with them as you would any other person. Don't condescend. Don't be mean. But do protect yourself.

If a ghost tries to harm you, tell it to behave and be prepared to take a stand. Remember, they are only spirits, while you have both a body and a spirit. You have more power than they do. Learn how to use it.

One approach in convincing a ghost to move on to its next phase of existence is to pull its memory back to the point of death. Ask specific questions. *What was your name? Where did you live? Were you married? Did you have any kids? What did you do for a living?* Those kinds of questions pull a ghost back to its last living memories. Once the ghost starts to remember who he or she used to be, then follow up with tougher questions. *How did you die? What year was it?* At this point, you should be able to talk the ghost into moving on to the next phase.

Some ghosts linger because of a fear of religious punishment. You cannot talk someone out of beliefs ingrained in life, but you can gently nudge them toward an honest assessment of the reality at hand. One way is to point out that lingering as a ghost creates a worse punishment for bad deeds than moving to the next incarnation.

The best advice to give a ghost is this: "Just let go."

* * * * *

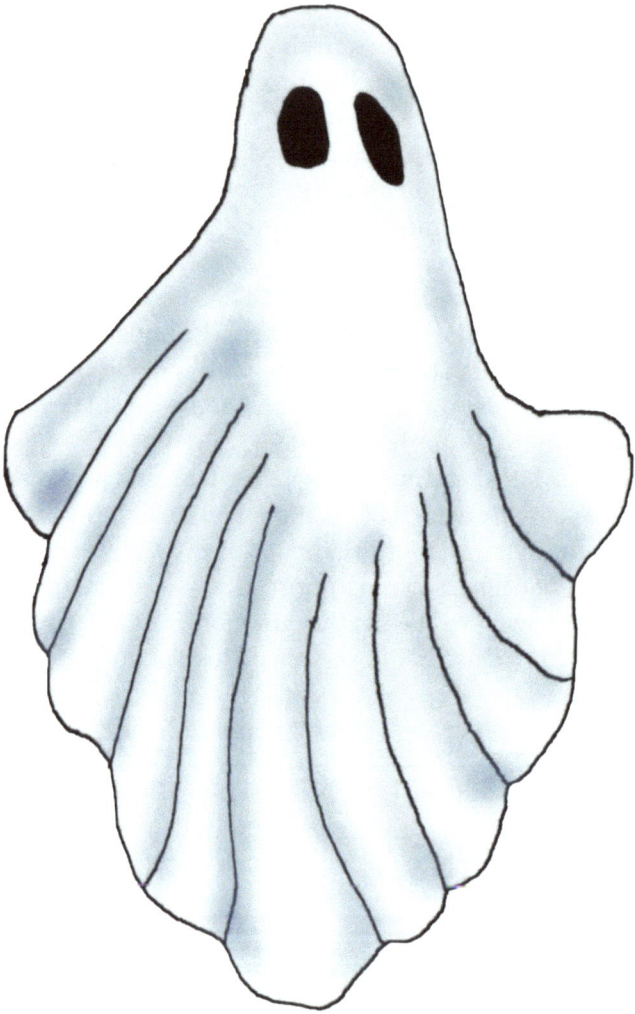

CHAPTER 11

Paranormal Tales

ALTHOUGH I infuse lots of ghosts and paranormal activities in my novels and short stories, those are pure fiction. However, below are a handful of true tales that touch on different aspects of the paranormal.

* * *

Granddad's Ghost

WHEN I was a teenager, my great-grandfather died suddenly one afternoon while working in the garden only steps from their farmhouse in rural Oklahoma. I grew up on that farm and for many years lived in that house with them.

Losing a loved one, even someone elderly, is always hard whether you are young or old. Despite my pleas otherwise, my parents forced me to stay alone in the upstairs bedroom that night.

The south window of that bedroom overlooked the garden where Granddad died. I knew what I would see as darkness enclosed.

As I stood looking out the window with only the stars for light, there was Granddad's ghost, standing in the garden with a smile and a wave.

The next instant he was standing inside the bedroom with me.

To be honest, I was terrified. I shouldn't have been, but I was. I jumped into that big old bed and pulled half a dozen handmade quilts over my head. Then I felt Granddad very gently tucking in the corners to keep me warm. Although that should have made me less afraid, at the time it did not.

I peeked out from under the covers once and saw Granddad standing vigil, leaning against the window in his lazy cowboy way with his arms crossed and one boot propped against the low windowsill.

It was a very long night, and I cannot say that I got any real sleep.

* * *

Kid's Table Ghost

KIDS often cannot distinguish living people from ghosts. They see deceased family members and continue to interact with them as they would any living person. As I discovered many years later, this occurred with me and several family ghosts.

One case in particular involved a great-grandfather on my mother's side. Once a year we would meet at a great-aunt's house, with relatives converging from all over Oklahoma and out of state.

When lots of relatives gather in a small house, one necessity is to set up a table for the kids, usually outside of the main dining room area. In this case, a small table was set up in what amounted to an enclosed porch turned laundry room.

One constant at these gatherings, at least from my perspective, was an old grandfather sitting on the inside steps to watch the children eat and visit. He never said a word, which today would have been my first clue, but as a child it just never occurred to me that anything was amiss. He would sit on the middle step, wearing a stained pair of overalls and a red plaid flannel shirt while smoking a crumpled old cigar.

Whenever I needed to run to the kitchen for something, I would stop at the bottom of the steps and say: "Excuse me." He would smile, get to his feet, and let me pass. That sounds like a living person, right? Not even close. I did not learn until well into adulthood that this particular grandfather had died in that house many years before I was born.

Even with all my experience dealing with ghosts in later years, until then I had no clue that some childhood memories might include a deceased family member – or two or three.

I once described this person in great detail to my mother, including his clothing and that old stinky cigar.

She had known her grandfather very well.

It was him, in ghostly form. No doubt about it.

* * *

Attic Ghost

WHEN I was four or five years old, my parents would take me to the farm of my father's grandparents.

My few memories of this particular great-grandmother were of a very old woman with long white hair, who rested on a parlor couch while wearing a nightgown and being covered with handmade quilts. She was very old, and I only saw her a few times before she passed.

However, it was not this great-grandmother who interacted with me. It was her husband, another great-grandfather. I remember seeing a very tall and handsome man with broad shoulders, silvery hair, and bright blue eyes. He wore a dark suit, plain but nice. He would stand at the end of the couch, stroking my grandmother's hair.

Then he would walk across the parlor and toggle a long finger at me. I would follow him up steep, winding stairs to a third story room, which was really an attic finished out into small bedrooms. In the south dormer, there was a pile of children's toys, mostly little metal tractors and like. He would sit on the hard wood floor and play with me, until my father yelled up the stairs that it was time to go.

As a child, you really don't make the connection that such playmates are ghosts. Sometimes they can move things, like small toys. Most of the time they don't speak aloud, but you hear them in your mind and don't make a conscious connection that the conversation is not occurring out loud. A small child simply does not catch such clues. They only react to love and attention. And I can assure you that this kindly old great-grandfather dearly loved me. And I him.

* * *

Mailbox Ghost

SEVERAL years ago, my husband and I used to take a specific back road through a rural area in order to avoid traffic.

As we turned off one country road onto another, to the right was an old and obviously empty homestead with the remnants of a large private garden beside a circa-1900 two-story wood-frame farmhouse.

The wood siding on the house was gray without any spec of paint remaining. The wraparound porch sagged in places and, even from the road, looked unsafe. No matter the time of day, there were never any lights shining inside the old house. No cars or trucks were parked in the driveway. There just was no sign of life from what once must have been a lovely home.

One afternoon with the sun shining brightly, we made the turn from one road to the other as usual and got a big surprise. Standing at the unpainted and somewhat tilted mailbox was an old woman. She just stood there looking at the mailbox, as if she did not quite know what to do. She was a very old woman, tall and rather thin. A multicolored knitted hat covered her head. She wore a dark shirt and dark pants with a lacy shawl pulled around thin shoulders.

Right after we passed the farmhouse, my husband asked if I saw the woman at the mailbox. I looked at him and said yes. Then I looked back down the road. The old woman was gone. There was no way she could have sprinted a hundred feet up that old pitted driveway.

No doubt about it. We had seen a ghost. And one who looked as solid and as real in the daylight as a living person.

A few months later my husband was visiting with a woman who worked in the same office as he did. She mentioned having problems selling the family homestead and told him where it was. Yes, it was that farmhouse.

My husband told his colleague what we had seen at the mailbox. Sure enough, we had seen her grandmother, who had been dead for several years.

"So that's why so many maintenance guys keep quitting," she said with a laugh.

* * *

Library Ghost

MANY years ago a friend of mine worked in a university library that was plagued with daily paranormal activity, one aspect of which had recently turned dangerous.

A ghost had figured out how to plug in the "book iron" at night, when everyone was gone. The librarians would show up in the morning to find that book iron red hot and ready to burn down the building.

My friend was at her wits end. She could not figure out which ghost in that massive building was the culprit and had no idea how to stop such dangerous activity.

First, I had her make a simple drawstring cloth bag to tie onto the big three-prong electrical plug at night. If the iron could not be plugged into the wall, then it could not be turned on. It was a simple solution that worked. No more early morning hot irons.

Next, we made a late afternoon trip to the library, just past closing time after everyone else had gone home, and went on a little ghost hunt.

As I walked off the back stairs of the third story, I spotted the culprit. Standing in front of that old book iron, with its electrical plug tied up in a nice new cloth bag, was a fairly solid apparition of a young man with shoulder length light brown hair and clothing that looked straight out of the 1970s hippie era.

"Can't get the bag off?" I asked him. I had to choke down a giggle. Seriously, it was just plain funny.

The ghost turned and looked at me. I'm not sure what surprised him more, that I could see him or that I had the gall to speak to him. After a moment, he uttered a squeak and zipped down the aisle out of view.

"Oh, no you don't," I said.

I ran down the aisle after him, while my friend headed down the adjacent aisle to keep him from doubling back. We cornered him at the end of the aisle, me on one side and she on the other. He squeaked again and vanished.

I don't know if he moved on, but he never tried to plug in the iron again and my friend never saw another glimpse of him. He could just have learned to hide from her.

Most ghosts are not accustomed to being either seen or chased, and certainly not scolded like naughty children. I have to admit that little ghost hunt was a lot of fun.

* * *

Office Elemental

YEARS ago I worked in a government office in northern Oklahoma City. The building was no more than perhaps twenty years old, so the last thing one would expect would be a serious paranormal infestation.

At it turned out, the building had been built on top of an elemental spirit, that was old, cranky, and extremely powerful.

It was impossible at that time to know what had been on the land prior to the construction of the building, but I got the feeling there had at one time in the very distant past been a water source of some kind.

What created the elemental was unknown, but it felt ancient. And it did not like having a building on top of it.

The three story building was octagonal in design with lots of glass and metal. On each of the three stories one office maintained a yellow appearance no matter how much lighting was added or what color the walls were painted. These small offices were stacked on top of each other, first floor to third floor, as if a column of dingy light arose from the ground beneath them. Every person who worked in one of those offices developed problems of some kind, from bouts of paranoia to much worse behavior. Most people assigned to those three offices either requested another office or wound up leaving the agency.

This particular elemental did not satisfy itself with tormenting only a few office workers. It played with the elevator, making it jerk and stall as if it might break its cables and fall. Most people who worked in the office learned to avoid the elevator. However, that then left them vulnerable to being tripped on the stairs.

A lot of trouble was stirred in that office. Some of it downright dangerous. People changed. Tempers flared. As much as I enjoyed my immediate co-workers and liked the work I was doing, I had to make a choice. To keep my job, I had to remain silent and not allow anyone to see me dealing with spiritual entities of any kind. That gave the old elemental a tremendous advantage over me.

Since I could not confront the elemental directly, I had to make a choice. After a couple of years, I quit my job.

On my last day there, I walked into the stairwell from the second floor landing and announced: "The building is yours. Do with it as you will. But if you follow me home, you will regret it."

I left it alone. It left me alone. A few short years later, the agency was moved to a different building across town.

What became of the elemental's building?

Last I knew, it was vacant.

* * *

The Little People

MANY Native American tribes have tales of the little people, which go by as many names as there are tribal languages. I just call them "kees," a term they seem to like.

My ancestry is mostly Cherokee and Choctaw with Scottish mixed in for good measure. Growing up, I heard lots of stories about the little people, from both the indigenous and the Celtic sides of the family.

What are the little people? The best answer I can give is that they appear to be nature spirits. Exactly what they are or how they come into being, I cannot say.

They inhabit wild wooded areas where there are sources of water nearby. As nature spirits, they are attracted to animals and especially like cats, both wild and domestic.

If you keep cats in your home and have woods nearby, you might attract the attention of little people.

These are sweet, gentle guardian nature spirits. If you pay attention to them, they will warn you of bad weather and even natural disasters.

Living in central Oklahoma, the threat of tornadoes is almost a year round thing, although more prevalent in spring and summer. I always know if a thunderstorm has a potential tornado threat, because the kees will gather in the house. They will tug on your pants leg. Poke the cat. If they have the strength, they might even turn lights on and off to get your attention. If kees are afraid of a storm, pay attention.

The weather in Oklahoma used to be confined to tornadoes and ice storms, but since November of 2011 earthquakes have been added to the list of natural hazards. Kees are wary of earthquakes. I'm not sure if that is fear, but they do tend to cluster inside the house several days before a new earthquake swarm starts.

During tornado season, it is hard now to know whether we are being warned about dangerous thunderstorms or coming earthquakes. Kees do not communicate telepathically, but they do convey emotions. They can appear as little two-legged fuzzy shadows moving through the house with about the same mass a large house cat.

Some kees can learn to move objects. The ones who do can be very mischievous. Playful, but never dangerous. One instance involved a set of glass kitchen countertop canisters.

My husband got up early one morning to head to work and found three glass canisters stacked upside down beside the coffeemaker, which was the first place he went upon rising. Figuring I had turned the canisters upside down for some reason unknown to him, he left them alone and headed to work.

I got up just a bit later and make my morning stumble into the kitchen. When I reached for the coffeepot, there were those old glass canisters stacked upside down on top of each other. In truth, the canisters were rather fragile and only used for storing various pastas. My first thought was that my husband had turned them upside down and must have had a good reason for it, so I left them alone.

When my husband returned home from work that afternoon, he made his way to the back bedroom where I do my computer work.

"What's the deal with the canisters?" he asked.

I looked up from the keyboard, puzzled by the question. "I was going to ask you the same thing."

It was his turn to look puzzled. "I found them stacked like that this morning and figured you must have gotten up in the middle of the night to do it."

"Nope," I replied. "Not me. I thought it was you."

He stood there a moment in his quiet Native American way. "Well, it seems someone likes to play games. The kees must have done it, but how did they do it without breaking those bases?"

"Apparently, with great care," I said. "Since those are your old canisters, they must have been telling you to be careful. Did you have any problems on the way to work?"

My husband looked a little startled. "Well, yes. There was a big wreck on the interstate, but it happened a few minutes before I got there."

"Just enough time for you to stop and ponder the canisters?" I asked.

"Yep, just about."

* * * * *

CHAPTER 12

Reincarnation Happens

REINCARNATION happens.

Spirits are called eternal souls for a reason.

One symbol for making a connection between the physical world and the psychic world is the dragonfly. A dragonfly goes through a unique life cycle. Its first incarnation is as a water nymph. Then it crawls onto land and spins a cocoon. After a while, it emerges as a new winged creature of the air. Because of this unusual transformational process, going from a creature of the water to one of the air, dragonflies are often associated with both reincarnation and psychic phenomena.

Another analogy is bumper cars. When I was a kid, I loved to visit the amusement park to ride the bumper cars. For those who don't know about bumper cars, they were shaped like little rounded carts with one small seat. Each car had a rod sticking up out of the back with a metal tongue that rode across a low metal ceiling. When the gate opened, everyone flooded across the floor to claim a car. You got in the seat and grabbed the wheel. When every car was full, the operator turned on a switch, electrifying the metal ceiling. A small amount of electricity flowed down the rod on each car, propelling it across the polished floor.

All you could do was steer. That's it. Just steer. Some turned their little cars as best they could to avoid being hit in an effort to get around the track. Most, however, turned their cars to bump into as many other cars as possible. Thus the term bumper cars.

I have always thought reincarnation was akin to riding the bumper cars. You wait in line. Rush to get a car. Sometimes you don't get one and wind up back at the end of the line, waiting for the next turn. When you are fortunate enough to snag a car, you have the choice of being a nice driver on the circuit or someone dedicated to mayhem. The choice is yours. You can navigate around tangles or create tangles on purpose.

Sometimes you make it around the track without any collisions. Sometimes you get whacked no matter what you do. Sometimes you are tempted to turn the wheel and do a little whacking yourself.

When you get aggressive in bumper cars, the usual result is getting tangled up in a pile by the wall with the rest of the aggressive drivers, and having to watch as other drivers zip past with waves and grins.

The old proverb "you reap what you sow" is the basic law of karma. Sometimes the rewards, be they good or bad, come quickly. Sometimes they don't come until the next incarnation. Sometimes things happen in this life with ties to past lives.

Is there a way to know why all things happen? No, and dwelling on that is a waste of precious time.

When you look inside and are honest with yourself, the answers usually will come. When they don't come, don't dwell on them. Just keep going.

Does everything happen for a reason? In my opinion the answer is no. Consider the bumper cars. Sometimes you get whacked without having done anything wrong.

Life is unpredictable. Good things rise over the hill like a warm sun. Bad things jump out from behind bushes to say *boo*. It does no good to dwell on whether you deserve the good or the bad.

Life is a journey. The better you are at taking life as it comes, the easier the journey is.

Avoid both complacency and isolation.

Life is meant to be lived.

And lived.

And lived again.

ABOUT THE AUTHOR

Terri Branson is an author, an editor, and a graphics artist. After earning an associate degree in math and science, she turned to the studies of creative writing and graphic design. Awards include the *EPPIE 2005 Best Children's Book Award* for the children's picture book, <u>Brother Dragon</u> and the *EPPIE 2004 Best Anthology Award* for the science fiction and fantasy collection, <u>Cosmic Sculpture</u>. Publications include adult coloring books, children's picture books, non-fiction, fantasy and paranormal short stories, romance novels, and science fiction novels. Terri lives in Oklahoma with her husband David. To read more about the author and see a current list of publications, visit her website at: <u>terribranson.com</u>.

* * * * *

ADULT PUBLICATIONS
By Terri Branson

A Psychic Life
Body, Mind, & Spirit (rated G)

Cosmic Sculpture
Science Fiction & Fantasy Anthology (rated PG)
EPPIE 2004 Best Anthology Award Winner

Dragon's Den
Science Fiction (rated PG)
[Also read inside *Cosmic Sculpture*]

Geodoodles
Adult Coloring Book (rated G)

Musk Rain
Paranormal Romance (rated PG)

Prairie Fire
Western Romance (rated PG)

* * * * *

CHILDREN'S BOOKS
By Terri Branson

A Very Dragon Christmas
Children's Picture Book (rated G)

Brother Dragon
Children's Picture Book (rated G)
EPPIE 2005 Best Children's Book Winner

Pete, the Peacock, Goes to the Zoo
Children's Picture Book (rated G)

Pete, the Peacock, Goes to Town
Children's Picture Book (rated G)

Scooter's World
Children's Picture Book (rated G)

Tyler on the Moon
Children's Picture Book (rated G)

Watch for Falling Rock
Children's Picture Book (rated G)

* * * * *

www.ingramcontent.com/pod-product-compliance
Lightning Source LLC
LaVergne TN
LVHW010023070426

835508LV00001B/28

9 781941 278642